Ezine Kaleidoscope December 2024

The Light in the Shadows

Ezine Kaleidoscope

Ezine Kaleidoscope

Volume 1 Issue 3 2024

Founder/Editor: Meetu Sehgal
Associate Editor: Chahat Singh
Cover Design: Tony
Graphic Design: Dilip Kumar
Digital Media Marketing: Raza Kamil
Business and Market Strategy: Ashi Sharma
Legal Advisor: Arushi Sharma

Owned by Meetu Sehgal
at S-423, Greater Kailash-I, New Delhi – 110048

Published by Notion Press

Contact Information
M: +91 9953753637
E: info@ezinekaleidoscope.com
W: www.EzineKaleidoscope.com

Table of Contents

From the Editor's Desk

Dear Reader,

The new age spirituality and our generic understanding of it usually focuses on the rosy aspects of spiritual life – being positive, not paying attention to the negative, letting the negative go, letting go of the darker aspects of our personality, and sometimes worse, suppressing the "so-called" negative emotions.

On the surface, it all sounds good. After all, who doesn't want to get rid of their negative emotions? However, there are two inherent problems with this thinking and approach.

This is not true spirituality. This is the opposite of it. Because spirituality never tells you to deny or suppress something. In fact, it is all about embracing everything – the good and the bad.

Denying, suppressing or wanting to get rid of parts of ourselves can cause more problems than creating solutions. Suppression or denial causes the problems to mutilate and show up in ways that are worse than the original problems. For example, suppressing the addiction to a substance, when not dealt with its root cause, can sometimes show up as an addiction to self-harm.

Therefore, in this December 2024 edition of Ezine Kaleidoscope, we bring you the theme of "The Light in the Shadows" which deals with the darker side of us, the sides hidden, the parts unseen and at times, the parts that we don't want to acknowledge because they are not pleasant enough.

You may be wondering why we chose this theme for the magazine this month because no one wants to talk about the negative stuff, it is difficult. And this is exactly the reason why we want to talk about this; we want to address the elephant in the room.

Diving Deeper in the Darkness

The so-called darker sides of us are the parts that feel anger, sadness, guilt, jealousy, envy, hatred, loathing, disgust, undeserving, unworthy, etc. They come up at the most unexpected moments when a friend talks about their success or happiness, when a neighbour buys a new car that you have been coveting for some time, when a colleague gets that promotion that you felt you deserved more, when a friend (who you secretly deep-down thought was ugly and awkward and would never find anyone) finds a boyfriend.

These are the moments when we want to deny that part of us that rises up, that feels those emotions we thought we never had or secretly never wanted to feel. It is these parts that we are looking at and addressing now.

A genuine question that may arise is why do we need to look at these parts of us; they are certainly not nice.

The answer to this is that the purpose of these parts has been to protect us, keep us safe and help us survive.

Keeping us Safe

At some point in our childhood, these emotions and parts of us that feel this were created as a defence mechanism to deal with our everyday reality and environment. A child doesn't have the mental and emotional resources to handle difficult situations or make sense of them. They tend to make sense of situations based on their limited understanding of the world and create behaviours and perceptions to help deal with such situations.

As we grow, those behaviours become embedded in our unconscious minds and we tend to forget where, when and why they were created. All we remember are the instinctive feelings and responses, that we often refer to as our basic nature.

These defence mechanisms are a great help to the child to help it survive and thrive. But for an adult, who has better emotional, mental and physical resources to deal with situations, these parts become more of a hurdle than a useful defence. They start to interfere in relationships with loved ones and the world around – with friends, colleagues, bosses, employees, etc. And because they are embedded deeply in the unconscious mind and often we are unaware of them (they are our blind spots), it becomes difficult to change them.

Shadow work is all about uncovering, recognizing, accepting and embracing these parts of us that we may or may not be familiar with, that were defence mechanisms at some point in time, and that cause us problems in our present day. Unless we do not embrace them, we can probably never heal them. Healing begins with acknowledging and accepting the problem.

In this edition, you will read about this theme from various perspectives, build bridges in your understanding of healing and spirituality and find a way ahead on your healing path.

Wishing you a beautiful December!

Light and Grace

Meetu Sehgal
Founder/Editor Ezine Kaleidoscope
Coach, Therapist, Healer and Tarot Reader

Uncovering the Unseen

Shadow Work with Journaling, Drama Therapy, and Vedic Insights

The concept of light and shadow within the psyche is a universal theme across cultures and philosophies, representing a duality that exists within every human being. In psychological terms, "light" symbolises our conscious, ideal self - the aspects we embrace and openly show to the world. "Shadow," a term popularised by Carl Jung, encompasses the hidden, repressed, or denied parts of ourselves that we may fear, dislike, or judge harshly. This journey to integrate our light and shadow aspects, often referred to as shadow work, is an essential practice for achieving self-awareness, compassion, and inner harmony.

What is Shadow Work?

Shadow work is a profound inner exploration aimed at uncovering the hidden, suppressed, or unconscious parts of our psyche. Coined by the Swiss psychoanalyst Carl Jung, the "shadow" refers to aspects of ourselves that we may deny, reject, or remain unaware of due to social conditioning, trauma, or internalised self-criticism. These hidden aspects can influence our behaviour, relationships, and mental well-being when left unaddressed. Shadow work invites us to explore these dimensions, allowing for healing and personal growth.

Understanding Light and Shadow in the Psyche

Light represents the qualities we accept and admire in ourselves—our strengths, virtues, talents, and socially acceptable behaviours. Shadow, however, includes characteristics we consider negative or unacceptable, often shaped by societal norms, personal traumas, and internalised beliefs. When we refuse to acknowledge our shadow, these qualities become powerful, unconscious forces that can negatively influence our thoughts, behaviours, and relationships.

Carl Jung proposed that ignoring the shadow self leads to "projection," where we see in others the flaws or fears we deny within ourselves. This projection can lead to judgement, conflict, and alienation. Integrating the shadow, on the other hand, promotes empathy, acceptance, and a richer, more complex understanding of ourselves and others.

Historical Background and Key Psychologists

The origins of shadow work are rooted in Jungian psychology. Carl Jung's studies in the early 20th century introduced the idea of the shadow as the "other side" of the self. Jung believed that integrating these parts through self-reflection and therapeutic practices is essential for achieving wholeness. He described shadow work as "the task of accepting our own evil and integrating it into our personality as a whole."

Freud, Jung's contemporary, also influenced shadow work through his ideas on repression and the unconscious mind. While Freud focused on hidden desires and traumas, Jung explored a more spiritual and holistic path, encompassing archetypes, the collective unconscious, and ultimately shadow integration.

In the late 20th and 21st centuries, psychologists such as John Bradshaw and Robert Bly expanded upon Jung's ideas. Bradshaw's book *Healing the Shame that Binds You* explores how shame creates shadows, while Bly's work in

A Little Book on the Human Shadow discusses how modern culture contributes to shadow repression.

Connections with the Vedas and Sanskrit Shlokas

The concept of the shadow isn't unique to Western psychology. In Vedic philosophy, the "shadow self" corresponds to concepts like "Maya" (illusion) and "Avidya" (ignorance). The shadow, in this context, represents the illusion of separation from the self and the universe, often leading to suffering. Through practices like meditation and self-inquiry, Vedic texts encourage inner work to transcend the illusions of the ego.

Consider the following shloka from the *Bhagavad Gita* (Chapter 6, Verse 5):

उद्धरेदात्मनात्मानं नात्मानमवसादयेत्।
आत्मैव ह्यात्मनो बन्धुरात्मैव रिपुरात्मनः॥

"One must elevate oneself by one's own mind, not degrade oneself. The mind is the friend of the conditioned soul, and his enemy as well."

This verse underscores the importance of self-awareness and the inner journey. The "enemy" in this context could be viewed as the shadow self, which hinders our growth if left unintegrated. Ancient Indian philosophy aligns with Jung's approach by emphasising self-acceptance, awareness, and transcendence.

Mythology and Archetypal Reflection

Exploring archetypes within mythology provides a safe distance from which to examine personal struggles. Myths from around the world depict journeys of light and shadow, which can inspire us and mirror our inner journeys.

In Indian mythology, for instance, the story of *Shiva*—the god who embodies both creation and destruction—symbolises the integration of opposites. Shiva's acceptance of his destructive and creative powers highlights the necessity of embracing all aspects of self for true balance.

Sanskrit Shloka from the Bhagavad Gita (Chapter 2, Verse 48):

योगस्थः कुरु कर्माणि सङ्गं त्यक्त्वा धनञ्जय।
सिद्ध्यसिद्ध्योः समो भूत्वा समत्वं योग उच्यते॥

"Perform your duty with a mind steady in yoga, renouncing attachment, and be the same in success or failure. Such equanimity is called yoga."

This shloka emphasises balance, reminding us that equanimity comes from integrating both success and failure, which could also be interpreted as the light and shadow within ourselves.

The Importance of Integrating Light and Shadow

1. **Emotional and Mental Wholeness** Integration brings us closer to a state of mental and emotional wholeness. Instead of denying or battling parts of ourselves, we learn to observe and accept them without judgement. This approach transforms our inner landscape, reducing inner conflicts and fostering peace.

2. **Increased Self-Awareness and Authenticity** Accepting our shadow encourages us to explore deeper motivations, hidden desires, and unconscious behaviours. By acknowledging our flaws and embracing our vulnerabilities, we gain insight into our true nature and can live more authentically.

3. **Enhanced Relationships and Compassion** Shadow integration makes us less judgmental and more empathetic. Recognizing our own imperfections allows us to accept others more easily, leading to healthier, more fulfilling relationships.

4. **Empowerment and Personal Growth** Once we accept our shadow, it no longer controls us. The energy used to suppress these aspects is freed, allowing us to use this newfound vitality to pursue our goals and dreams.

Shadow Work through Journaling

Journaling offers a structured way to engage with our shadows. It allows us to record thoughts, reactions, and feelings that emerge during reflection. By observing recurring themes, we begin to recognize hidden patterns and suppressed emotions.

Techniques for Shadow Journaling:

1. **Prompt Writing:** Begin by asking yourself questions such as, "What am I most ashamed of?" or "What beliefs hold me back?" These prompts encourage honest self-reflection.
2. **Mind Mapping:** Identify a particular emotion or behaviour you're curious about, then create a mind map of associated thoughts and memories.
3. **Letters to the Shadow Self:** Writing letters to parts of yourself, especially those you reject or dislike, can reveal hidden fears and desires. This compassionate dialogue fosters self-acceptance.

Expressive Arts Therapy in Shadow Work

Expressive arts therapy integrates various art forms, including visual art, drama, and movement, as therapeutic tools to access emotions beyond verbal expression. Art allows us to externalise inner conflicts and bring our shadows into the open.

Key Techniques:

1. **Abstract Drawing:** Creating abstract shapes or figures that represent suppressed feelings can help us visualise our shadow self.
2. **Movement and Dance:** Freeform movement to express feelings often buried inside provides a physical and emotional release, accessing parts of the shadow that may not easily surface through language.
3. **Mask-making:** Designing a mask that represents your shadow can bring to light hidden traits, allowing for self-reflection upon completion.

Drama Therapy and Tale Therapy in Shadow Work

Drama and tale therapy are particularly effective in shadow work because they involve role-playing and narrative construction, allowing us to explore different aspects of ourselves.

1. **Drama Therapy:** This therapeutic form leverages role-play, storytelling, and character exploration to engage the shadow. The Indian classical dance forms, particularly Kathakali and Bharatanatyam, embody archetypal expressions of good and evil,

light and shadow, providing a medium to process complex emotions.

2. **Tale Therapy:** Storytelling, especially using mythology and folk tales, reveals universal themes that resonate with our shadows. In Indian mythology, figures like Shiva embody both the creator and destroyer archetypes, presenting a symbolic balance of the shadow and light within. In storytelling sessions, participants can explore their shadows by connecting with these mythic symbols, allowing for personal reflection and resonance.

The Roots and Significance of Shadow Work with Indian Performing Arts

Indian classical performing arts like Kathakali, Bharatanatyam, and Koodiyattam embody the duality of light and shadow through their complex narratives and intense emotional expressions. These forms often depict conflicts between opposing archetypes, reflecting themes of inner conflict and resolution. By adopting these classical art forms, one can personify the shadow, thus engaging deeply with hidden aspects of the self.

For example, the *abhinaya* (expression) in Bharatanatyam conveys emotions that may mirror our inner fears, anger, or sorrow, acting as a safe vessel for catharsis. Through dance or drama, shadow elements such as guilt, regret, or grief find expression, bringing release and insight to the practitioner.

Guided Self-Compassion Exercises

Self-compassion is essential for shadow integration. Exercises that encourage self-love and kindness allow us to embrace our shadow with compassion, rather than rejection.

Self-Compassion Exercise:

- Place a hand over your heart and gently acknowledge any feelings of discomfort related to your shadow. Repeat affirmations such as, "I am worthy of love and acceptance in all my forms."

Affirmations for Integration

Affirmations focused on acceptance and unity can gradually reshape our attitudes toward our shadow. By repeating these affirmations, we reinforce the belief that all parts of ourselves are valuable.

Examples:

- "I embrace all aspects of myself with kindness and curiosity."
- "I allow my shadow to teach me about my strengths and vulnerabilities."

The Transformational Outcome of Light and Shadow Integration

Integrating light and shadow helps us transcend superficial dualities, leading to a more profound, nuanced experience of life. We become more resilient, self-aware, and compassionate, both toward ourselves and others. Shadow work doesn't mean eliminating all negative traits; rather, it invites us to see ourselves as multifaceted beings capable of growth and transformation. Each part of us holds lessons that, when embraced, create a unique tapestry of strength, vulnerability, and authenticity.

About the Writer

Ashi Sharma is a multi-faceted professional and an inspiring force in the realms of personal development and holistic healing. As an author, expressive arts therapy practitioner, EFT practitioner, tarot healer, and podcaster at Breaking Mythos, she brings a unique blend of insights to her work as a Reiki master, lifestyle and business coach and consultant. She has been honoured in the BW Wellbeing World 30 Under 30 Awards for the years 2022 and 2023. Her latest work is part of a beautiful coffee table book, 'Mythology' enriched with hand-painted illustrations that bring ancient stories and legends to life. In this book, she talks about the spiritual journeys of Shukracharya and Odin.

Beyond the Shadows

How Nature and Reflection Guide Us to Inner Healing

There are moments in life when we unexpectedly receive wisdom from the most unusual places. Sometimes it's a random memory, sometimes nature, and at other times, a quiet reflection with a cup of coffee. Today, I'd like to share some reflections that came to me, as if the universe gently whispered them in my ear.

Reflecting on the Past: The Elephant's Lesson

While sipping my coffee one day, I was taken on a journey down memory lane. I recalled a time in kindergarten when I saw an elephant up close, with its massive ears flapping slowly. To a child, the sight of such a large, gentle creature was overwhelming. Even now, as I watch wildlife documentaries, the elephant continues to teach me valuable lessons.

One interesting thing about elephants is that they are among the few animals that cannot see their whole body. It is as if they are unaware of their vastness. This made me think: How often do we, too, miss seeing our worth and strength? We become so caught up in the past, in problems and issues that once seemed so significant but have long since faded. These past challenges, much like the bubbling of hot water, only seem intense in the moment but eventually evaporate, leaving no trace behind. So, why do we hold on to the burdens of past events, whether good or bad, when they no longer serve us?

This simple realization from observing an elephant can transform our lives. We must learn to let go of our past, release those emotions, and travel lightly on this journey called life. Each day is a new opportunity to move forward without carrying the weight of what has already passed.

Mirror Reflections: Facing Our Insecurities

Studies have shown that when an elephant sees its reflection in a mirror, it becomes visibly agitated. At first glance, this might seem like a trivial fact, but it holds a powerful lesson for us. When we look into the mirror of life, when we encounter situations that trigger us, it's often because we are confronting our own fears and insecurities.

We tend to project these inner conflicts onto others, becoming irritated or frustrated by what we perceive in them. But in reality, it's our own unresolved emotions and fears that we're grappling with. This is a humbling realization, one that teaches us to look inward for peace instead of blaming others for our discomfort.

Working on ourselves is no small feat—it requires tremendous effort and courage. But as we begin this inner work, peeling back the layers of societal expectations, past conditioning, and personal trauma, we slowly start to rediscover our authentic selves. This journey to self-awareness and self-love is the foundation of true healing. Only when we embrace who we are at the core can we find clarity and peace in our daily lives.

The Importance of Stillness and Self-Reflection

In this fast-paced world, finding time to be still is a luxury many overlook. Yet, stillness is the key to understanding the purpose of life. We are not here to rush from one task to another. Instead, we are here to live with intention, to discover what truly brings us joy, and to understand the deeper purpose of our existence.

Take a moment to sit with yourself and ask, "What makes me happy? What is the purpose of my life? Why am I here on Earth?" These questions may not have immediate answers, but with patience and regular self-reflection, your soul will start to reveal its secrets. The journey of self-discovery is not a sprint; it's a slow, gentle walk toward truth.

One analogy that resonates deeply is the story of the deer and the leopard. Though the deer is much faster, it often falls prey to the leopard. Why? Because the deer frequently looks back in fear, losing focus on its escape. The leopard, on the other hand, despite its slower speed, stays focused and determined, and this focus enables it to succeed.

This teaches us that fear can hold us back more than any external limitation. If we stay focused on our goals and stop letting fear and distractions cloud our vision, we can achieve what we are truly capable of.

Healing: Embracing the Pain for Growth

Imagine for a moment a sword piercing through your body. It hurts, doesn't it? But now imagine someone trying to remove that sword. That process also causes pain, but it's a different kind of pain—the pain of healing. Healing, my dear ones, is not an easy process. It's painful, but it's necessary to prevent deeper emotional wounds, what we can call the "fungus" of unresolved hurt.

If you look at your shadows as challenges, they will seem like the obstacles of your life. But if we shift our perspective, these shadows can become tools of strength. It's like Arjuna from the Mahabharata, who was able to shoot the fish by focusing solely on its eye. The message here is clear: if we channel our energy in the right direction, undistracted by doubts or fears, we can hit our target.

We all have fears and insecurities. Instead of letting them paralyze us, let's make them our bow and arrow. Fear can propel us to take brave actions, and our insecurities, once confronted, can give us the courage to grow. Aim with confidence at your true purpose, and pursue it with a smiling attitude, humbleness, and an unwavering belief in yourself.

When we allow time and the universe to heal us, we experience pain, but it's the pain of growth, of removing the sword that has caused so much suffering. Yes, it's difficult to stand still and witness this process. But with trust, patience, and a willingness to heal, we can eventually emerge stronger, wiser, and free from the emotional burdens that once weighed us down.

Trust in the Universe: Let Time Heal the Wounds

We often rush the healing process, hoping that by doing something—anything—we can make the pain go away faster. But healing is not something we can force. It's a slow, organic process that requires trust in the universe, and patience with ourselves.

When we allow the universe to do its work, when we choose the right path and stay true to it, the healing will happen. One day, you will look back and thank yourself for enduring the pain, for not giving in to fear or doubt. You will realize that there are higher powers supporting you, and they will catch you when you fall.

Silence: The Key to Unlocking Inner Wisdom

In the chaos of life, silence becomes a rare but invaluable gift. It is in silence that we can hear the voice of our inner consciousness, the soft yet powerful guide that knows our true purpose. This voice is often drowned out by the noise of daily life, but when we sit in stillness, we can finally hear its wisdom.

Make friends with silence. It is through those quiet moments of reflection that we can observe our thoughts, our actions, and our deepest desires. Yes, it takes courage to sit with yourself, to be still and listen, but I promise you—it is worth it. In these moments of silence, you will uncover the answers you've been searching for.

Final Thoughts: Embrace the Journey

Remember, my dear ones, life is not a race. It's a journey of self-discovery, healing, and growth. Along the way, you will face challenges, but each challenge is an opportunity to learn, to grow, and to uncover more of your true self. Trust the process, trust the universe, and most importantly, trust yourself.

About the Writer

 Bhawna is a gifted intuitive and mystic with a lifelong connection to the spiritual realm. From a young age, she demonstrated a unique sensitivity to energies and a natural ability to distinguish clarity from confusion, a gift her family recognized early on. With a postgraduate degree and a thriving professional career, Bhawna followed her true calling to support others, using her intuitive insights and spiritual tools to guide people through life's challenges. Known by some as a prodigy in the mystical arts, Bhawna's journey has led her to explore diverse spiritual tools and practices, from Energy Aura Reading to Akashic Records Reading, Tarot, Chakra balancing, and Rune interpretation. She also deeply understands the Law of Attraction and how it can empower and transform lives. She uses these tools now to help others find peace and purpose by bringing light to their shadowed paths and transforming negative situations into growth opportunities.

Exploring Darkness as a Pathway to Healing and Self-Discovery

In the quiet of the darkness, when all light appears to fade, there is a place that many of us fear to enter. It's a place where shadows linger—shadows of the past, of unresolved pain, and of parts of ourselves we struggle to accept. Yet within this darkness lies a hidden light—a spark of spiritual awakening and profound healing.

The image above—a solitary figure illuminated within a vast expanse of shadow—perfectly captures the essence of this personal journey. Standing alone, surrounded by darkness, the figure appears small and vulnerable, yet resilient. A beam of light shines down, casting a long shadow, representing both the past and the aspects of the self that are often hidden from view. This powerful visual serves as a reminder that, while we may walk through shadows, we can also find light within them.

The Shadows of the Past: Uncovering the Lessons We Carry

Understanding How Past Experiences Shape Who We Are

We each carry within us the shadows of the past. These shadows are formed by memories, choices, and experiences that linger within us, shaping who we are in ways we're often unaware of Many of these shadows arise from wounds—emotional traumas, unprocessed grief, or mistakes we wish we could undo. For some, these shadows represent guilt or shame; for others, they are the remnants of lost dreams or unfulfilled potential.

Even though these shadows might look frightening, they hold valuable lessons for us. Our past experiences have formed the core of our being, shaping our perspectives, values, and responses to the world. Embracing these shadows doesn't mean condoning past mistakes or reopening old wounds, but rather understanding them and how they still affect us. When we turn to face these parts of ourselves, we can start to unravel the reasons behind our actions, beliefs, and fears. In the process, we unlock a new level of self-awareness and healing.

Imagine the solitary figure in the image. That individual could be each of us, standing at the edge of a vast internal landscape. The shadows on the ground aren't just random distortions—they are reflections of our inner selves. The darkness that surrounds us isn't an enemy; it's more like a mirror, showing us the parts of ourselves we haven't yet fully understood or accepted. By standing within this darkness, we gain an opportunity to reclaim lost fragments of our identity and turn past wounds into sources of wisdom.

The Challenges of Human Life: Finding Strength in Adversity

Life is rarely an uninterrupted journey of ease and joy. Instead, it is often filled with challenges, pain, and moments of despair. These difficult times can feel like dark clouds obscuring our inner light, leaving us lost and unsure of our path. Yet, the spiritual journey teaches us that adversity is not something to fear or avoid; rather, it is a teacher, guiding us toward deeper levels of understanding and resilience.

In spirituality, there is a concept, that light and darkness are not mutually exclusive. Just as a candle's flame shines brightest in the dark, so too can our souls find strength in times of hardship. The challenges we face—whether they are moments of grief, feelings of inadequacy, or periods of uncertainty—are invitations to grow. They invite us to dive deep, to confront what scares us, and to emerge stronger and wiser.

In the image, the figure stands alone, enveloped by darkness yet illuminated by a single beam of light. This visual symbolizes the potential we all have to stand strong, even when surrounded by life's uncertainties. The light does not completely dispel the shadows, but it offers a guiding presence, a reminder that we are not alone in our struggles. As we learn to accept and embrace life's challenges, we find within ourselves a wellspring of strength we may never have known existed.

Embracing the Shadow Self: The Path to Wholeness

Integrating All Parts of Ourselves for Authentic Living

Carl Jung, a pioneer in psychology, introduced the idea of the "shadow self"—the hidden, often suppressed aspects of our personality. The shadow self is composed of traits and desires we might deem unacceptable, traits we'd rather others never see. It is the part of us that feels jealousy, anger, or fear, and the one we try to mask with positivity or self-control. Yet, no matter how hard we try to push these parts away, they remain, influencing our behaviour in unconscious ways.

Spirituality teaches us that true wholeness requires us to integrate all aspects of ourselves, even those we find uncomfortable or undesirable. **In many ways, the journey of spiritual growth is not about becoming "perfect" but rather about becoming whole.** This involves acknowledging the existence of our shadow selves and embracing them with compassion and understanding.

The shadow in the image is an extension of the figure, inseparable from its form. This symbolizes that our shadow self is a part of who we are. To deny its existence would be to deny a fundamental part of our humanity. By embracing our shadow, we give ourselves permission to be fully authentic. We become more forgiving, not just of others but also of ourselves. This acceptance does not mean giving in to every impulse but rather acknowledging these impulses without any shame or judgment.

Through shadow work—a process that involves exploring and understanding these hidden parts of ourselves—we can heal wounds, release long-held fears, and free ourselves from the unconscious patterns that limit our lives. In the light of self-awareness, we see our shadow selves clearly, not as threats but as parts of ourselves that need healing and integration.

Uncovering the Divine Spark That Guides Us Through Darkness

At the core of our being is a light that is pure, unchanging, and eternal. This light is often described as the soul, the higher self, or the divine spark within. When we journey through darkness, this inner light guides us forward, offering hope and clarity even in the face of despair.

This light, however, can be obscured by layers of conditioning, trauma, and limiting beliefs. As we work through our shadows, we peel back these layers, revealing the light that has always been there, patiently waiting for us to rediscover it. The figure in the image, standing beneath a radiant beam, symbolizes this discovery. Though surrounded by shadows, they are also illuminated, a testament to the resilience of the human spirit and the profound capacity for healing and transformation.

Many spiritual traditions speak of this light as a connection to the divine. In Christianity, it is often referred to as the "light of God." In Hinduism, the Atman, or soul, is seen as a spark of the divine presence within each individual. In Buddhism, enlightenment is the ultimate realization of this inner light, a state where one transcends both light and dark to experience unity and peace.

Practical Steps for Embracing the Light in the Shadows

To truly embrace the light within the shadows, we must engage in practices that promote self-reflection, healing, and spiritual growth. Here are some ways to begin this journey:

1. **Journaling**: Writing about our thoughts, fears, and emotions helps us gain clarity. It can be a safe space to explore our shadow selves and uncover patterns that need healing.

2. **Meditation**: Mindfulness meditation allows us to observe our thoughts without judgment. With regular practice, we can become aware of our unconscious habits and slowly let them go.

3. **Therapy or Counseling**: Sometimes, we need support to work through past trauma or understand our shadow. Speaking with a therapist can provide guidance and insight, helping us uncover aspects of ourselves we might be avoiding.

4. **Spiritual Practice**: Engaging in spiritual practices such as prayer, ritual, or contemplation can help us connect with our inner light and find strength in times of darkness.

5. **Self-Compassion**: Shadow work requires self-compassion. We must learn to forgive ourselves, accept our imperfections, and treat ourselves with kindness.

Walking the Path Between Light and Dark with an Open Heart

In the end, the journey of embracing the light within the shadows is one of self-discovery and integration. The figure in the image represents each of us as we stand between light and dark, finding balance, peace, and understanding. By facing our shadows, we gain insight into who we truly are. By embracing our imperfections, we discover the profound beauty of our humanity.

Spiritual growth is not a path to perfection but a path to wholeness. When we accept the shadows within us, we allow our inner light to shine brighter. And when we walk through the darkness with an open heart, we realize there is nothing to fear because we carry the light within that will lead us home.

About the Writer

I'm Dilip Kumar, a dedicated freelancer with a passion for visual storytelling through photography, videography, video editing, and graphic design. Photography is my true calling—I love capturing the beauty of nature and the raw emotions of people in every frame. My work combines creativity and technical skill to create images and visuals that resonate deeply with viewers.

The Three Pillars of Healing
Resilience, Self-Love, and Acceptance

Life is full of highs and lows—moments of light and stretches of darkness that sometimes feel impossible to face. Most of us instinctively try to dodge the difficult parts, maybe pretending we're okay when we're not or hiding our pain because it feels too big to share. But here's the thing: happiness and healing often hide in those very shadows. Real, lasting healing means we face our struggles, practice self-love, and build up resilience, even when it feels impossible.

In this piece, we'll explore how to find light in the darkness, how to fully accept ourselves, and how to build resilience that lasts.

Finding Light in the Darkness

When life feels like it's pulling us under, it's easy to get lost in negative feelings. Sometimes, we get so caught up in our sadness or stress that we convince ourselves not to ask for help. Reaching out can feel like admitting weakness or can seem too complicated when we're in the thick of it. But sometimes, reaching out can be one of the bravest things we do.

In moments like these, I think of a twist on Dumbledore's words:

"Hope and help are closer than we think if we can just find the courage to look for them."

Seeking support, whether from a friend, therapist, or even through journaling, is a step toward finding that light.

And if you're someone who is doing okay right now, remember that someone out there might need a little encouragement. Sometimes, being open about our own struggles or just offering a listening ear can make a huge difference. We all have the capacity to be the light someone else is looking for.

Embracing Self-Love, Bit by Bit

Self-love might sound like a trendy buzzword, but at its heart, it's about learning to treat ourselves with kindness. It doesn't mean ignoring our flaws or acting like we're always happy— it's about giving ourselves the compassion and understanding we'd give a friend. When we cultivate self-love, we start to build the strength to face life's challenges with a little more courage.

Here are a few simple ways to practice self-love:

1. **Practice Positive Self-Talk:** Try being mindful of how you talk to yourself. If you catch yourself being critical, try swapping those thoughts for affirmations or a few gentle reminders of your worth.

2. **Set Boundaries:** Self-love sometimes means saying "no" to people or situations that drain us. Recognizing our limits and setting boundaries is a powerful way to protect our mental and emotional well-being.

3. **Engage in Self-Care:** Whether it's getting enough rest, eating nourishing foods, or taking breaks to recharge, self-care is a core part of self-love. Caring for our bodies and

minds sends a message that we are worth that attention and care.

4. **Forgive Yourself:** We're all human, and we all make mistakes. Loving yourself means letting go of past regrets and focusing on learning and growing rather than dwelling on perfection.

Building Lasting Resilience, Step by Step

Resilience isn't just about "bouncing back." It's the ability to adapt to whatever life throws at us, to grow through hard times, and to keep moving forward. Being resilient doesn't mean we're unaffected by challenges; it's about how we handle them and learn to move through them.

How to Build Resilience When Things Get Tough

Building resilience is a lifelong process, but there are ways to strengthen it bit by bit:

1. **Focus on Growth:** When setbacks come, it's natural to feel defeated. But try to look for the lessons in these moments. Challenges and failures often teach us the most valuable lessons.

2. **Lean on Your Support System:** Whether it's friends, family, or a community, having people to lean on makes a huge difference. Remember, asking for support is a sign of strength, not weakness.

3. **Stay Present:** Practicing mindfulness helps us stay grounded in the present. When we're not caught up in regrets or worrying about the future, we're better able to face whatever life brings with clarity.

4. **Be Flexible:** Life doesn't always go as planned, and that's okay. Resilience is about being willing to adapt when things go sideways and find ways to move forward, even when it's not easy.

5. **Celebrate Progress**: Take time to acknowledge your own resilience, no matter how small your progress may seem. Every step forward is a reminder of your strength and your ability to get through hard times.

Healing: A Journey That's Far from Linear

Healing isn't a straight line. Some days we feel like we're moving forward, and on others, we might feel like we're back at square one. Healing is often slow, filled with moments of growth, setbacks, and the occasional breakthrough. But the most important thing is to keep going, even when progress feels slow.

When we commit to healing, we start to see life differently, realizing that each struggle we face can be a stepping stone toward growth. Healing asks us to face the parts of ourselves we'd rather avoid and to process our emotions instead of ignoring them. By working through these feelings, we make space for new growth, and, bit by bit, we begin to see light in places we once thought were only shadows.

Leading by example is one of the most powerful ways to help others find their light. When we model self-love, prioritize our healing, and demonstrate resilience, we encourage others to do the same. In a world that often pressurizes us to appear perfect, showing our authentic, imperfect selves is a radical, freeing act.

Embracing Both Darkness and Light

The journey to self-love, healing, and resilience is a journey back to ourselves. It's about embracing both our strengths and our weaknesses, the light and the shadows within us. By nurturing self-love, we build a strong foundation for healing. By cultivating resilience, we give ourselves the tools to handle life's inevitable challenges. And by facing our shadows, we discover the light we didn't even know was there.

Healing doesn't mean we erase our pain or pretend it doesn't exist. Instead, it's about learning to live alongside our pain, to understand it, and to grow through it. The light in the shadows is there for all of us to find. With patience, courage, and compassion, we can step into our fullness, finding balance in the beautiful, imperfect mess of who we are.

Taking a Step Toward Light and Healing

So take it one step at a time. Keep going, even when it's hard. Find courage in reaching out and be open to the support that others are willing to offer. Remember, in embracing both the light and the dark, we build lives that are richer, more resilient, and more meaningful.

About the Writer

Anandmai Kumar is the Founder of The Purple Lotus Foundation and the Managing Partner of Soul Shine Pvt. Ltd. A compassionate and dedicated individual, she is committed to healing and empowering others. As an internationally certified life coach, NLP practitioner, and expert in a variety of energy and scientific healing therapies—including Tarot, Reiki, and Emotional Freedom Technique—Anandmai has developed a holistic approach to well-being. She specializes in personalized coaching that helps clients unlock their intuitive potential, guiding them toward a harmonious balance of mind, body, and soul. Since 2014, her transformative work has touched the lives of countless individuals, rejuvenating their spirits and fostering lasting healing.

Self-Boundaries

When the Hardest Limits Are the Ones We Set for Ourselves

Sometimes boundaries may look a lot different than we expected. It isn't a clearly defined thing you see. It depends on the situation. *How do I know?* Well, I was tested and tried until I learned my lesson, just like everyone else. No biggie! So, how different are we talking about? Well, sometimes boundaries may not only have to be created externally, as with other people; they may have to be created with ourselves too.

Umm..what?

I know, I know. Y'all are thinking I have gone mad. How can boundaries exist with ourselves? Take for instance, you know you have an important meeting the next day and you know if you went for that friend's birthday, you'll definitely end up coming home late and even worse, may end up drinking, which means not only will you be late the next morning, you might be in the worst possible hangover, thanks to those extra tequila shots in the end after a night filled with cognac and rum.

However, on the other hand, if you don't go and perhaps book a lunch for another day with your friends, not only will you make it for your interview, you might just win on every front.

Difference?

Well, I'd give you a hint. It starts with a 'B' and ends with an 'S'.

That's right!

It's you setting **'boundaries'** for yourself. I'm well aware some people would like to call it 'disciplining yourself' or 'a routine' and I hear you, I support you. Yes, those are indeed very much within the purview of 'boundaries' in my understanding. Boundaries with yourself can also involve saying 'No' to things that may affect your future in a bad way. It also includes taking yourself to places that may not be comfortable but necessary for your growth and hence one day when...

A part of me wanted to believe that this is it.
Perhaps, it is over after all.
Maybe two people with immense attraction and good compatibility don't have to end up together all the time.
Maybe it was a lie all along.

My head wouldn't shut up. The constant chatter was killing everything. I could barely eat and yet when I looked at him, I saw nothing. No signs of empathy. *Was he that good at masking?* Not a clue! No matter how much time you spend with someone, I suppose you can never really know them completely. Why? Well, because they're changing with time and so are you.

He was changing. Not sure why though.

Till yesterday he was my best friend. Today he looked like a monster gobbling up the burger right after telling me he has feelings for me and that he still cannot break up with his girlfriend.

Are people allowed to do that? Can people legally do that? Mess with everyone's head around because they can't afford to lose a single soul. They're scared of being alone. Why me, God why me?

I was still stoned. Opened my mouth but couldn't utter anything. I stuttered. Words escape me sometimes you see. I tried to feel something. Focus on the wind. Focus on the lights. *Nothing!* It's like my whole body created a shield to protect me from getting hurt. But, I was already hurt. I opened my mouth again but only 'umm... Umm... that... Umm...' fell out and once again, I couldn't talk. He stared blankly at me. I couldn't even look him in the eyes. But I could feel his gaze.

As soon as he finished his food, I got up. 'Let's pay and leave? I think I'm late for bed. Got an early morning tomorrow.' I darted for the door as if I didn't even want to hear what more he had to say.

What on Earth could he possibly have to say now? What? That he will marry us both if he could but he doesn't have a choice? What?

I looked at the yellow tree one last time outside his house before hugging him goodbye and darted like I was being chased by monsters. I literally flew all the way home.

Three days passed. Did he break up? No.
Five days passed. A week. A month.
No breakup.
Was I friends with him?
Not a chance!

One thing I learned from this experience was that no matter how important that friendship was to me or the fact that we both had feelings for each other; I wouldn't settle for anything less than what I deserved. It wasn't about what was in front of me. A perfect partner. A soulmate. We had the same interests. Same way of looking at the world. Easygoing. Caring. Kind. But the fact that he wasn't ready to let go of his past to have a future with me bothered me. On some level, it would have always bothered me if we had continued. Did I want to lead a life like that? Definitely not!

***

It wasn't about two people falling in love. Sometimes love stories aren't that simple. And that's okay. Maybe some people simply walk into our lives to teach us how to love ourselves better. How their screwing up can be a useful lesson for us to love ourselves enough to let them go, is definitely a journey worth doing.

I am Samara. Maybe even you are. Perhaps we all have been in her place one day or another. Boundaries may take a conscious assessment and effort to know what's really going on and how one can set them in order to function better and to preserve our energies. But if something doesn't feel right, chances are it isn't. It wasn't easy for me to let go of a good friend. It never is. But setting that boundary was necessary. Simply not reaching out anymore or allowing them access to me was a part of this process. I knew I was capable of finding and having better friendships where love was reciprocated. Where nothing was forced and it just flowed.

If you liked this story and would love to know more about boundaries, subscribe to Kaleidoscope Ezine today!

About the writer

Arushi is a PhD candidate in Law at Trinity College Dublin and her research work revolves around Data Protection in the financial sector. A full-time law student and a part-time energy worker, she is passionate about teaching and learning. With more than 7 years of experience in healing, she firmly believes in the transformative power of self-reflection and the guidance that each healing offers. Her offerings as a healer and coach help individuals navigate challenges and confidently embrace opportunities.

Have you ever noticed how stepping outside our comfort zone can feel overwhelming, even frightening? It's not uncommon to experience a mix of emotions when we consider moving away from the familiar and into the unknown. Often, at the heart of these emotions is a sense of vulnerability, a feeling that can hold us back just when we're contemplating something new, exciting, or challenging.

The Oxford English Dictionary defines vulnerability as "the quality or state of being exposed to the possibility of being attacked or harmed, either physically or emotionally." While you may be reading this in a safe environment, comfortably shielded from physical harm, vulnerability most often impacts us emotionally, where the risks are felt deeply and personally. When we explore why vulnerability feels so daunting, we find it is tied to a variety of powerful emotions.

The Emotions That Hold Us Back
Weight of Perception and Exposure

The fear of how others perceive us or the thought of being judged for expressing our genuine thoughts, values, or beliefs can be intimidating. The vulnerability of putting our true selves out there, even though something as simple as speaking or posting online, invites the possibility of scrutiny. Next is the feeling of embarrassment, another potent emotion that few of us willingly choose to experience. Who would want to risk being in a situation where we could feel humiliated or exposed?

Fear of Failure and loss

Often, success is seen in terms of achieving specific goals, recognition, or rewards. When these tangible markers are missing, it can be easy to fall into the emotion of feeling like a failure. This fear can be a considerable barrier to taking risks, even when the outcomes might lead to personal growth. And of course, there is the fear of loss—the fear of losing something or someone we deeply value. Whether it's a cherished relationship, a secure job, or a sense of self-worth, opening ourselves up emotionally can sometimes feel like risking everything we hold dear.

Uncovering the Roots of Vulnerability

When we think about vulnerability, we might recognize these emotions as shadows of past experiences. Think back to childhood: maybe there was a moment when you stepped out of your comfort zone, only to face criticism, mockery, or even a lack of acknowledgment, leaving you feeling exposed. These early experiences often shape our responses to vulnerability, and over time, we may start building walls to keep from experiencing that pain again.
However, there's an empowering way forward. By learning to identify, acknowledge, and act upon our emotions, we can begin to work through the discomfort that accompanies vulnerability, finding resilience and self-acceptance along the way.

Turning Vulnerability into a Source of Strength

A Three-Step Approach: Identify, Acknowledge, Act

Identify- Recognizing Emotional Triggers

The first step is to identify what we're feeling. Imagine yourself in a scenario that makes you uncomfortable—maybe it's speaking in public, sharing your artwork, or simply voicing an unpopular opinion. Pay attention to your feelings. Perhaps you feel a tightening in your chest or a knot in your stomach. These physical cues can help you recognize the underlying emotion, which often links back to past experiences.

Acknowledge: Validating Our Emotions

Once you've identified what you're feeling, the next step is acknowledgment or acceptance. It's easy to identify a feeling and then push it aside, carrying on as though it doesn't matter. But acknowledgment is a powerful step in embracing vulnerability. By recognizing your feelings without any judgment, you validate your experience and allow yourself to be fully present in that moment. This might be as simple as taking a deep breath, closing your eyes, and saying to yourself, "IT'S OKAY" Let yourself feel where the emotion sits within you, and remind yourself that this feeling doesn't have to be a barrier.

Act: Cultivating Empowering Responses

Finally, it's time to act. Acting on an emotion doesn't mean reacting impulsively at the moment; rather, it's about cultivating a response that allows you to approach similar situations with greater ease in the future. For example, if speaking in public makes you nervous, acknowledge that it's okay to feel that way. The next step is to prepare yourself to feel more comfortable the next time around, perhaps by practicing, seeking feedback, or envisioning a positive outcome. Small, intentional steps can create a foundation of confidence that empowers you to face similar situations with more comfort.

Finding Support in the Journey

If working through emotions alone feels overwhelming, remember that there are many tools available to support your journey. Speaking with a therapist or counsellor can provide invaluable insights, helping you navigate the complex emotional landscape of vulnerability. A professional can guide you through unresolved emotions that may be holding you back, assisting you in developing strategies to manage life's challenging moments with greater confidence and resilience.

Moving Beyond Fear to Embrace Vulnerability

Each of us will experience vulnerability differently depending on our unique circumstances and past experiences. However, by identifying the emotions that make us uncomfortable, acknowledging their presence, and acting on them in ways that support our growth, we can begin to step out of the shadow of fear. Vulnerability, once an obstacle, can become a gateway to connection, confidence, and self-acceptance. By embracing this journey, we allow ourselves to live more fully, moving forward with a deeper sense of love for who we are and all we're capable of becoming.

About the Writer

Shweta is a gentle soul, passionate about animals, sustainability and authenticity. She believes in living with honest ideals and helps individuals, both personally and professionally, to uplift their energies and achieve their highest potential. Having managed huge projects for major NGOs, she also provides her services as a life coach, EFT practitioner and animal communicator. She also runs an animal shelter that takes care of wounded and abandoned pets, strays, and old community animals.

The Sacral Chakra

Unlocking Creativity, Sensuality, and Emotional Healing

The seven chakras are associated with different aspects of our personality, emotions, or physical functions.

In the previous edition, we discussed the first Chakra- the Root Chakra. In this edition, we will explore the Sacral Chakra, located in the lower abdomen, which is the second chakra of the energy body. It governs creativity, sexuality, and passion and is often associated with emotional and physical healing.

The Sanskrit word **Svadhisthana** means, "dwelling place of the self". So, your Svadhisthana is where you reside in your body. It's also known as the Sacral Chakra because it's located about two inches below the navel in the lower abdomen. The Sacral Chakra governs our creativity, sexuality, pleasure, and sensuality.

Understanding the Basics of Svadhisthana

Svadhisthana means one's place or one's abode. It's all about enjoying life and going with the flow. It's where we truly feel at home in our bodies and at peace with ourselves. This chakra is about feeling grounded in who you are as a sexual being, enjoying pleasure, connecting with others, feeling creative, and experiencing joy. This is also related to self-expression and confidence.

By being aware of the internal processes and patterns that drive our behaviours, we can effectively manage our emotions and work through any challenges. Whether we embrace a more spiritual path or explore more worldly experiences, staying attuned to our Svadhisthana chakra will help us lead a vibrant life full of creativity and joy.

Location and Physical Connections of Svadhisthana

The Svadhisthana is located in the sacrum, a small triangular-shaped bone at the base of the spine. The sacral plexus, a network of nerves that innervates the lower abdomen and pelvis, is also located in this area.

The subtle body is also linked to Svadhisthana, and this chakra corresponds with many internal organs in the lower abdomen, including the bladder, kidneys, and reproductive organs. This chakra also governs the lymphatic system, a network of tissues and organs that fight infection and remove waste from the body. As one of the most important energetic centres in the body, Svadhisthana plays a crucial role in our physical, mental, and emotional health.

Symbols, Colour, and Element: A Deeper Look into Svadhisthana

The **orange colour** is associated with Svadhisthana, which represents creativity and vitality. Orange represents many facets of our being -- from physical vitality and strength to creativity and passion. Whether we are engaging in artistic expression, exploring new ideas, or simply engaging in movement and activity, the power of Svadhisthana helps us bring our ideas to life and manifest them into reality.

The element associated with Svadhisthana is **water**. Water is essential for all life on earth, providing nutrients, cooling us down in summer heat, and making plant growth possible.

The Subconscious Mind and Emotional Expression

Svadhisthana is a gateway to the subconscious mind and our more primal impulses. It governs many aspects of our lives that we are not even aware of, such as sexual desires, creativity, and emotions. When Svadhisthana is out of balance, we could find ourselves consumed by our  primal impulses and unable to control our emotions and behaviour. However, when this chakra is in balance, we harness the powerful energies associated with it to bring our latent talents and desires to fruition. Whether through artistic expression, physical activity, or sexual intimacy, Svadhisthana is responsible for helping us unleash our creative potential and enjoy the fullness of life in all its aspects.

This chakra is not only about physical pleasures but is also responsible for our ability to connect with others emotionally and helps us forge stronger and more meaningful connections, bringing us a greater sense of fulfilment in our relationships. Our sense of smell, taste, sight, touch, and hearing are all governed by the Svadhisthana chakra. When this chakra is out of balance, we find ourselves disconnected from our senses or unable to enjoy the full range of sensations life offers.

This energy center is essential to connect with your five senses, and when it is balanced, you open yourself up to a greater range of sensory experiences. A balanced Svadhisthana is also the cause of greater peace and contentment in life.

Blocked or Imbalanced Sacral Chakra

- A blocked Sacral Chakra manifests as
- Creative stagnation,
- Sexual dysfunction,
- Low self-esteem
- Bladder infections and kidney problems,
- Menstrual problems,
- Infertility and low libido,
- Addictions.
- Childhood trauma or sexual abuse can also lead to a negative attitude towards sexuality or intimacy and thus block Sacral Chakra.

Symptoms Of a Weak Sacral Chakra

- Feeling disconnected from your emotions, leading to numbness and loneliness.
- Difficulty in expressing your emotions openly or be creative in your pursuits.
- Health issues like menstrual problems, infertility and low libido, fluid retention, and being overly emotional or sexual.
- Prone to addictions or self-destructive behaviours.
- It can also make you more susceptible to addictions or activities to fill the emptiness or vacuum you're feeling inside.

- You feel creatively blocked or find it hard to enjoy your hobbies and interests.

Causes of an imbalanced Sacral Chakra.

1. Lack of physical affection in childhood. If you were not given enough hugs or affection as a child, it could have led to feelings of deep Insecurity and a belief that you are not worthy of love. This can block your ability to experience pleasure and creativity as an adult.
2. Sexual, emotional, or physical trauma.
3. Constantly suppressing your creativity or sexuality can also lead to an imbalanced Sacral Chakra. If you have been repressing your true desires for a long time, it is important to start exploring these feelings to help align your chakra.

Restoring Harmony in the Sacral Chakra

Affirmations to Unblock and Empower Svadhisthana

1. I am creative and I express my creativity in all that I do.
2. I am confident and comfortable in my skin.
3. I am worthy of love, respect, and happiness.
4. I love and approve of myself just the way I am.
5. The beej mantra *"Vam"* is the Sanskrit mantra for the Sacral Chakra, which means "water". It represents the chakra's fluid, creative energy.

6. Hand mudras related to Sacral Chakra are **Yoni Mudra** (the gesture of the universal womb) and **Varun Mudra** (the gesture of water).

Crystals, Essential Oils, and Food for Sacral Chakra Healing

Sacral Chakra healing uses crystals in many different ways. Like using crystals in meditation, carrying them with you, placing them directly on the body, or wearing them in the form of a bracelet. Some of these crystals are Carnelian, Snowflake Obsidian, Citrine, and Amber.

Essential oils for Sacral Chakra are Jasmine, Ylang-ylang, Sweet Orange, Tangerine, etc. Foods related to Sacral Chakra are oranges, carrots, peaches, papaya, and sweet potatoes.

Practices to Awaken Your Sacral Chakra

- Spend time near water bodies, like lakes or oceans,
- Meditate on the colour orange. Wear/use orange colour in the form of foods associated with water, like cucumbers, and oranges.
- Practice Yoga, massage treatment, and deep breathing techniques.

Engage in creative pursuits like painting or journaling and transmute the energy of the Sacral Chakra.

About the Writer

Prathma is an expert in various methods of "Wellbeing and Alternative Healing" Modalities. She has been practising & teaching Reiki & other healing Modalities since 1999. A teacher of love and self-acceptance, she brings light and optimism to anyone who meets her. She believes in a holistic approach with a combination and different healing modalities where intuition and logic, science and spirituality go hand-in-hand. Her simplicity and expertise makes the techniques work like powerful charms that have been helping thousands of people around the globe.

Clearing the Path

December's Gift of Reflection and Emotional Release

December, as the final month of the year, carries a unique energy that encourages reflection, rest, and renewal. This time offers an opportunity to pause, heal, and clear away emotional and mental burdens before stepping into a new beginning. From a holistic health standpoint, engaging in inner healing work during December can significantly impact well-being by fostering a fresh, unburdened start to the coming year. This is why it is the perfect month to start some deep cleansing with 'Shadow Work'.

Here's why this month is especially conducive to inner healing and how it can enhance holistic health.

1. A Season for Reflection and Release

December's colder days and longer nights (in many parts of the world) naturally invite a slower pace and introspection. As daylight diminishes, we are drawn inward, mirroring nature's cycle of quiet dormancy. This rhythm aligns with the inner healing process, which benefits from an environment of calm and contemplation. By reflecting on the past year, you can identify areas of unresolved emotional pain, unprocessed memories, or limiting beliefs that may be weighing you down.

Tips:

- **Daily Journaling:** Dedicate a few minutes each day to reflect on personal challenges, triumphs, and areas of growth over the past year.
- **Gratitude and Release Ceremony:** Write down what you are grateful for as well as what you'd like to release. Letting go of what no longer serves you

helps create space for new opportunities and growth in the year ahead.

2. Clearing Emotional Energy

During December, we naturally crave warmth and comfort, both physically and emotionally. As a season tied to holiday gatherings and festivities, it can also stir up memories, nostalgia, and sometimes unresolved family dynamics. This can be the perfect time to address any old wounds, mend relationships, or find peace within yourself. Inner healing practices help us to identify emotions that may have been repressed or overlooked during the busyness of the year.

Tips:

- **Meditative Visualisation:** Imagine releasing past emotional baggage in a calm, visualised setting.
- **Heart-Centred Practices:** Practices like loving-kindness meditation or heart coherence exercises are gentle ways to restore emotional balance and bring warmth to any old or painful memories that arise.

3. Preparing for New Beginnings

As December marks both an ending and a beginning, it is a powerful time for setting intentions for the new year. However, to set meaningful, grounded intentions, it's essential to start with a clear and healed inner foundation. Unresolved inner conflicts or limiting beliefs can hinder our ability to move forward with clarity and confidence. Engaging in inner healing helps clarify your values and desires, making space for intentions that truly align with your authentic self.

Tips:

- **Forgiveness Rituals:** Forgive yourself or others for past hurts, allowing you to enter the new year unburdened.
- **Intentions Setting:** Focus on intentions rooted in self-compassion and inner peace rather than external achievements. A balanced inner state is the best starting point for personal goals.

4. Strengthening the Immune System and Physical Health

Holistic health considers the mind-body connection fundamental to wellness. December's colder temperatures and heightened stress from holiday preparations can strain the immune system. Unresolved emotional issues can add to this stress, making us more vulnerable to physical illness. Inner healing reduces stress and supports immunity, enhancing overall resilience during winter's colder months.

Tips:

- **Breathwork and Grounding Exercises:** Regular breathwork or grounding exercises help regulate stress responses, supporting immune function.
- **Mindful Movement:** Gentle yoga or stretching routines can aid in releasing stored tension, while also promoting physical relaxation and well-being.

5. Embracing Solitude and Self-Care

December provides a natural pause for self-care, encouraging moments of solitude that nurture healing and self-awareness. These quiet moments can be used to listen to your inner voice and needs, which are often drowned out by the demands of daily life. This intentional self-care can set a strong, positive tone for the new year, reinforcing your commitment to holistic health.

Tips:

- **Create a Sacred Space:** Set up a peaceful area for meditation, journaling, or simply resting. A calm environment can amplify the healing benefits of solitude.
- **Self-Care Practices:** Engage in self-care activities that nourish both body and soul, such as taking warm baths, reading inspirational books, or enjoying herbal teas.

6. Aligning with Nature's Rhythm

From a holistic health perspective, December's natural cycle of hibernation and withdrawal parallels the inner work of healing and self-nurturing. Tuning into this rhythm fosters a harmonious connection with both nature and ourselves. Rather than pushing for external achievements, the energy of December encourages us to let go, relax, and prepare for renewal. By aligning our inner healing work with this seasonal cycle, we can enter the new year feeling aligned and rejuvenated.

About the Writer

Ashi Sharma is a multi-faceted professional and an inspiring force in the realms of personal development and holistic healing. As an author, expressive arts therapy practitioner, EFT practitioner, tarot healer, and podcaster at Breaking Mythos, she brings a unique blend of insights to her work as a Reiki master, lifestyle and business coach and consultant. She has been honoured in the BW Wellbeing World 30 Under 30 Awards for the year 2022 and 2023. Her latest work is part of a beautiful coffee table book, 'Mythology' enriched with hand-painted illustrations that bring ancient stories and legends to life. In this book, she talks about the spiritual journeys of Shukracharya and Odin.

Tips for Winter Solstice
Embracing Tranquility and Joy

When the night is the longest, it is time for the body and mind to hibernate. Well, not in a bear sense. But hibernation for humans holds a different and important significance.

Winter solstice is the celestial phenomenon when the night is the longest and the day is the shortest. It usually occurs on 21-22 December in the Northern Hemisphere, when the sun reaches its southernmost point. This celestial event heralds the return of longer days and the promise of renewal. This time holds a unique magic that has captivated civilizations throughout history.

1. Connecting with Nature

- **Witness the Sunrise**
  One of the most magical aspects of the winter solstice is the sunrise. Set your alarm early and find a serene location to witness the first light of the day. This simple act can be a powerful way to connect with nature and welcome the returning sun.
- **Nature Walks and Hikes**
  Embrace the tranquility of winter by taking nature walks or hikes. The stillness of the season can be meditative, providing an opportunity to reflect and find solace in the beauty of a snow-covered landscape.

2. Creating a Cozy Atmosphere

- **Warmth in Decor**
  Bring warmth into your home by adorning it with a cosy decor. Consider using warm-toned throws, cushions, and candles to create a snug

atmosphere. Adding a touch of winter-themed decorations can enhance the festive spirit.

- **Hygge Practices**
Embrace the Danish concept of hygge, which is all about creating a feeling of coziness and contentment. Light a fire, enjoy a cup of hot cocoa, and surround yourself with soft blankets for an evening filled with comfort.

3. Nourishing Your Body and Soul

- **Seasonal Foods**
Indulge in seasonal foods that not only nourish your body but also celebrate the flavours of winter. Opt for hearty stews, root vegetables, and spices that evoke the essence of the season.
- **Tea Rituals**
Create a soothing tea ritual to warm yourself from the inside out. Explore a variety of herbal teas and take the time to savour the flavours, allowing the ritual to become a mindful practice.

4. Reflecting and Setting Intentions

- **Journaling**
Take advantage of the solstice's reflective energy by journaling. Reflect on the past year, expressing gratitude for its lessons and setting positive intentions for the coming months.
- **Meditation and Mindfulness**
Engage in meditation and mindfulness practices to center yourself during this introspective time. Connect with your breath, embrace stillness, and

let go of any negativity, making space for new beginnings.

- **Crafting and DIY Projects**
  Engage in creative endeavors by crafting winter solstice-themed decorations or making handmade gifts. These activities not only channel your creativity but also add a personal touch to the season.

Conclusion

As the winter solstice graces us with its quiet beauty, there are countless ways to celebrate and embrace its magic. From connecting with nature and creating a cosy atmosphere at home to nourishing your body and soul and reflecting on the past year, these tips for winter solstice offer a holistic approach to making the most of this special time. So, bundle up, sip on some warm tea, and let the enchantment of the winter solstice fill your heart with tranquillity and joy.

About the Writer

Meetu Sehgal is a Personal Transformation and Emotional Wellness Coach, EFT Trainer, Tarot Reader, Author, Reiki Grandmaster and Counselling Psychologist. With more than 15 years of experience in her field, she has been passionately working with individuals, helping them resolve health, wealth and relationship challenges through coaching. Meetu Sehgal is an MBA graduate from Delhi University and also holds a Masters in Psychology. Passionate about writing and spirituality, she has blended both in her work, which has helped hundreds of people around the world find peace within themselves. Her latest book, "Happy Inside Out", is a definitive guide to understanding and handling emotions and moods.

Winter Wellness

Nutritional Secrets for Mental Well-being

The winter months are challenging for mental health. As December brings shorter days and colder weather, it's crucial to leverage nutrition to manage moods and emotions effectively. This article explores how specific foods can influence mental well-being, provides recipes for better weight management, and discusses hormonal aspects affecting women's mood during winter.

The Connection Between Food and Mood

Numerous studies suggest that diet significantly impacts mental health. Nutrients like omega-3 fatty acids, complex carbohydrates, and vitamins B and D play crucial roles in brain function and mood regulation. A well-balanced diet can help mitigate symptoms of anxiety and depression, particularly during darker months when seasonal affective disorder (SAD) is more prevalent.

Millennials and Gen Z

Millennials and Gen-Z are particularly vulnerable to mood disorders. According to the American Psychological Association, these generations report higher levels of anxiety, depression, and stress compared to older generations. Contributing factors include economic instability, social media pressure, and global uncertainty. Nutrition can serve as a valuable tool in managing these stressors.

Hormones, Mood, and Winter: Nutritional Tips for Women

Women's hormonal fluctuations can significantly impact mood, especially in winter when vitamin D levels drop due to less sunlight exposure. Here are key aspects and tips to manage these changes.

1) Estrogen and progesterone Balance

- **Impact** – Fluctuations in these hormones can lead to mood swings, anxiety, and depression.
- **Nutritional tip** – Incorporate foods rich in phytoestrogens like flaxseeds, soy, and legumes to help balance hormonal levels.

2) Serotonin production

- **Impact** – Lower levels of sunlight can reduce serotonin production, a neurotransmitter crucial for mood regulation.
- **Nutritional Tip** –Consume tryptophan-rich food such as turkey, eggs, and cheese to boost serotonin levels.

3) Blood Sugar Stability

- **Impact** – hormonal changes can affect insulin sensitivity, leading to blood sugar spikes and crashes.
- **Nutritional Tip** – Opt for complex carbohydrates like whole grains, pulses, oats, ragi, and barley, which provide sustained energy and help stabilize blood sugar levels.

4) Iron Levels

- **Impact** – Iron deficiency, common in women, can lead to fatigue and mood disturbances.
- **Nutritional Tip** – Include iron-rich food such as lean meats, spinach, and lentils. Pair with vitamin C-rich food to enhance iron absorption.

5) Hydration

- **Impact** – Dehydration can lead to symptoms like depression and anxiety.
- **Nutritional Tip** – Drink plenty of water and include hydrating foods like cucumbers, oranges, and watermelon.

Simple Recipes for Healthier Moods and Weight

Overnight Soaked Oats Recipe

- Take oats, chia seeds, and yogurt (optional) in a lidded container or jar.
- Pour in the almond milk, and stir thoroughly to combine. Make sure that there are no clumps of chia seeds around the bottom or sides of the jar!
- Cover and store overnight in the fridge.
- When you're ready to eat, give the oats another stir, add your desired toppings, and enjoy!

Green Salad Recipe

Ingredients
- 1 cup mixed greens
- 1 cup baby spinach leaves

- ⅓ cup cucumber, sliced
- ⅓ cup carrot, shredded
- ⅓ cup red bell pepper, diced
- 3 oz sliced baked tofu
- ¼ cup sun-dried tomatoes, roughly chopped
- 1½ tbsp pepitas(pumpkin seeds)
- 2 tbsp basil leaves, chopped
- ⅓ cup baked chickpeas

Dressing
- 1 tbsp olive oil
- ½ tbsp lemon juice
- ½ tsp Dijon mustard
- Salt & pepper to taste

Directions
1. Put all your mixed greens and spinach in a large bowl.
2. Add cucumbers, carrots, bell peppers, and tomatoes.
3. Put in the protein of your choice.
4. Top with the tasty toppings, i.e., pumpkin seeds, basil leaves, and chickpeas.
5. In a separate bowl, place all dressing ingredients and whisk until combined.
6. Toss all the salad ingredients in a medium bowl.
7. Dress and plate your salad.

Kodo Millet Upma Recipe

Ingredients
- 1/4 cup kodo millet (25g - 30g)
- 1 tbsp ghee or oil

- 1 tsp mustard seeds
- 1 tsp urad dal
- 2 green chillies
- 1 medium onion
- 1 small carrot
- ¼ cup pea (boil)
- 10 curry leaves
- 2 cup water
- Salt as per taste
- Handful of coriander leaves
- 1 tsp lemon juice

How to Prepare

- Wash and soak Kodo Millet in water for 30 minutes, then drain and set it aside.
- Heat ghee/oil in a pan, add mustard seeds and urad dal and fry until golden brown.
- Now add chopped green chilli, curry leaves, and chopped onions to the pan. Sauté the onion till it gets translucent, and then add chopped carrot and peas.
- Sauté for a few minutes, then add turmeric powder, and salt, and mix well.
- Add soaked millet to the pan, and mix everything well.
- Pour 2 cups of water into the same pan and bring it to a boil) and cook for at least 15 minutes.
- Garnish it with chopped coriander and squeeze lemon juice (optional).

Chicken Soup Recipe

Ingredients

- 1 whole chicken, cut into pieces
- 9 cup water
- 2 large carrots
- 2 celery sticks
- 1 large onion
- 3 garlic cloves
- 1 bay leaf
- 1 tsp dried thyme
- Salt and pepper as per taste
- Fresh parsley, chopped for garnish

Preparations

- In a pan, add water and chicken pieces, and place the lid to bring it to a boil.
- Add bay leaf and dried thyme into the pan and let it simmer for 30 minutes until the chicken gets cooked.
- Remove the chicken pieces from the pan carefully and let it cool, then remove the bay leaf.
- Once cooled, shred the chicken meat and discard the skin and bones.
- Add vegetables—carrot, onion, celery, and garlic to the pan and cover it to let the vegetables simmer for 20 minutes.
- Add salt and pepper as per taste.
- Put the soup into a bowl and garnish it with fresh parsley.

Steamed Fish Recipe

Ingredients

- 1 whole fish, clean it

- 2-3 minced garlic cloves
- 1 inch piece of ginger
- 2-3 green onions
- 1 tbsp sesame oil
- 1 tbsp veg. oil
- Salt & pepper to taste
- Lemon

Prepare the fish

Pat the fish dry with paper towels, and make 2-3 diagonal slashes on each side of the fish for even cooking and season it with salt & pepper.

Prepare steaming setup

- Bring water to a boil in a steamer or a pot.
- Stuff some ginger and green onions into the cavities of the fish, and place the fish on a heatproof plate that fits in your steamer or pot.
- Once the water starts to boil, place the fish plate on the steamer rack, cover it, and let it steam for 10 minutes depending on the fish's size. The fish will be well-cooked when the flesh easily flakes with the fork.
- While the fish is steaming, heat some vegetable oil in a small saucepan on medium heat, add ginger, and garlic and sauté well. Bring the mixture to a gentle simmer and remove it from heat. Stir 1 tbsp sesame oil, and your sauce is ready.

Once the fish is done, remove the plate from the steamer, pour the sauce over the fish and sprinkle some green onions on the top to garnish. Serve the fish with lemon.

About the Writer

With over seven years of experience, Swati Bhutani is a certified dietician known for her expertise in therapeutic diets and weight management. She blends clinical nutrition with Ayurvedic principles to create personalized wellness plans that address individual health needs. Holding a Postgraduate Diploma in Dietetics and Public Health Nutrition from Lady Irwin College and a Fellowship in Clinical Nutrition from Apollo Hospitals, she is skilled in managing conditions like diabetes, cardiovascular health, and hormonal balance. Through a compassionate, sustainable approach, she empowers clients to achieve lasting well-being.

Tarot Predictions for December 2024: A Guide for All Zodiac Signs

Aries (March 21 - April 19): Two of Swords

Career & Finances:
The Two of Swords suggests a period of indecision or being at a crossroads in your professional life. You may face a tough decision that requires careful thought. This could relate to a job offer, a project you're unsure about, or a conflict with a colleague. The key here is to trust your intuition and take your time before making any major decisions. Avoid rushing, as clarity will come when you give yourself space to think.

Love & Relationships:
This month you might be dealing with a situation where you need to make an important choice, possibly between two people or two directions in your relationship. If you're single, this could also mean you're torn between pursuing

a potential relationship or staying single. Take the time to understand your feelings and what's truly best for you.

Health:
In terms of health, the Two of Swords points to a need for balance and mental clarity. You may be feeling mentally drained or confused about your health choices. It's important to evaluate whether stress or mental overwhelm is affecting your physical well-being. Practice mindfulness and avoid making any hasty decisions.

Taurus (April 20 - May 20): Four of Cups

Career & Finances:
The Four of Cups reflects a sense of dissatisfaction or boredom in your professional life. You might be feeling uninspired or disconnected from your work. Opportunities may present themselves, but you're either not interested or are too focused on what's not working. To improve your career prospects, try to open yourself up to new possibilities, even if they don't seem perfect at first.

Sometimes the best opportunities come in unexpected forms.

Love & Relationships:
If you're in a relationship, you may feel distant from your partner or as if something is missing. For singles, this card can indicate a feeling of being stuck in the past, unable to move forward emotionally. Take some time to reflect on what you truly want and try to embrace the present moment. New love may be on the horizon, but you need to be emotionally available to receive it.

Health:
You may be taking your health for granted or not addressing issues that have been building up. This month, focus on reconnecting with your health through mindful practices like yoga, meditation, or simply paying attention to your body's needs. It's time to break out of any unhealthy habits that are holding you back.

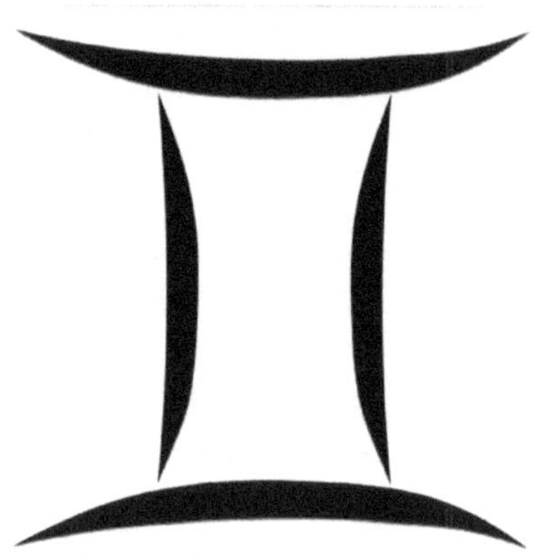

Gemini (May 21 - June 20): Nine of Wands

Career & Finances:
The Nine of Wands shows that you're nearing the end of a difficult period in your career. You've worked hard, and though you might feel worn out or exhausted, you are resilient and capable of overcoming any final obstacles. Stay determined, as your hard work is about to pay off. Keep a positive mindset and don't let setbacks discourage you.

Love & Relationships:
In relationships, the Nine of Wands suggests that you've been through a lot and are feeling protective of yourself. Whether you're single or in a relationship, you may feel guarded or wary due to past experiences. This card asks you to stay strong and persevere through any emotional challenges. Trust that you are capable of healing and that better days are ahead.

Health:
Health-wise, the Nine of Wands indicates that you might be feeling physically or mentally drained. You've been pushing yourself hard, and it's important to take a break and allow your body to rest. Don't be afraid to ask for support if you need it, whether from a medical professional or loved ones. Remember, self-care is essential to keep going.

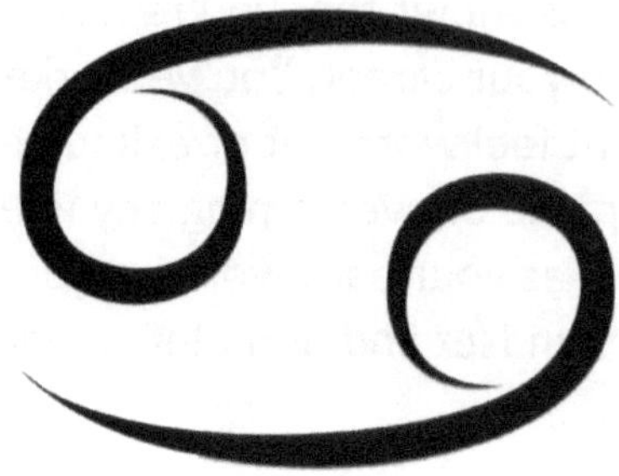

Cancer (June 21 - July 22): The Lovers

Career & Finances:
The Lovers card is a powerful card of alignment, choice, and harmony. In terms of career, this card suggests a decision that aligns with your true passions. You might find yourself making an important choice that could significantly shape your professional future. There could also be a collaboration or partnership that will benefit you greatly, whether it's with a colleague or a business venture.

Love & Relationships:
In love, The Lovers signifies deep connection and partnership. If you're in a relationship, this is a time for growth and intimacy. You may find that you and your partner are more in sync than ever before, and it's a great time for making long-term commitments. For singles, you could meet someone who feels like a soulmate. Pay attention to the connections that feel truly meaningful, as they could be life-changing.

Health:
When it comes to health, The Lovers encourages balance. Your physical and mental well-being are inextricably linked, so make sure you're taking care of both. You may feel more motivated to adopt a holistic approach to your health, such as combining physical exercise with mental wellness practices like meditation or therapy. Trust your body's wisdom and make decisions that honour your well-being.

Leo (July 23 - August 22): Five of Pentacles

Career & Finances:
The Five of Pentacles often signifies a sense of lack or financial hardship. You may be feeling the weight of financial stress, or perhaps your work situation is leaving you feeling undervalued. However, this card also suggests that help may be closer than you think. Reach out to others if you need support—whether it's career advice, financial guidance, or simply a sympathetic ear. The Five of Pentacles is a reminder that struggles are temporary, and there's always a way to turn things around.

Love & Relationships:
In love, the Five of Pentacles suggests feelings of loneliness or being emotionally abandoned. If you're in a relationship, you might feel neglected or unsupported. For singles, you may be going through a period of emotional isolation. It's important to address these feelings and be open to receiving help and love from others. You don't have to face these challenges alone.

Health:
When it comes to your health, the Five of Pentacles warns you not to neglect your physical or mental well-being. You might be feeling run-down or isolated, which can take a toll on your health. Take time to nurture yourself, whether through rest, self-care, or seeking professional guidance. Don't hesitate to ask for help if you're struggling.

Virgo (August 23 - September 22): Two of Pentacles

Career & Finances:
The Two of Pentacles indicates a period of balancing multiple responsibilities, possibly at work or in your finances. You may feel like you're juggling several projects or financial commitments at once, and it's important to stay organized and manage your time well. Although it might feel overwhelming, you have the skills to handle everything that's on your plate. Prioritize wisely and ask for help if needed.

Love & Relationships:
In relationships, the Two of Pentacles suggests the need for balance. You may find yourself trying to balance time between a partner, family, and your own needs. For singles, you could be juggling multiple options or trying to find time for love amidst other commitments. It's important to maintain harmony and not let one area of your life overwhelm the others.

Health:
The Two of Pentacles in health shows that you may be juggling different aspects of your well-being, such as work, exercise, and personal time. Don't neglect your health while managing other parts of your life. It's crucial to find a routine that supports both your physical and emotional well-being. Make sure you're giving yourself time to rest and recharge.

Libra (September 23 - October 22): Queen of Swords

Career & Finances:
In your career, December holds the potential for a breakthrough. The Queen of Swords suggests a period where your communication and leadership skills will shine. You might find yourself taking a more authoritative stance or handling difficult conversations with tact and precision. Financially, this is a time for practical decision-making.

Love & Relationships:
In matters of the heart, the Queen of Swords indicates that transparency will be key. If you're in a relationship, it's a time for clearing the air and addressing any misunderstandings. If there have been lingering doubts or uncertainties, you'll be able to see the truth clearly and communicate what you need with compassion but also with firmness. For single Librans, you may find yourself attracting individuals who value intelligence, honesty, and authenticity.

Health:
The Queen of Swords suggests that your physical well-being is closely tied to your mental state. It's a great time to engage in activities that clear your mind, such as meditation, journaling, or even a digital detox. Consider setting boundaries around your mental load, ensuring that you're not overwhelming yourself with unnecessary stress.

Scorpio (October 23 - November 21): King of Wands

Career & Finances:
The King of Wands suggests you're stepping into a position of authority or taking charge of a big project. Your confidence and passion will inspire others, and you may have the opportunity to showcase your leadership skills. Financially, this is a good time to take bold steps towards increasing your income or starting a new venture.

Love & Relationships:
In relationships, you may find yourself taking a more

dominant role or feeling the need to lead. It's important to balance your assertiveness with compassion, so you don't unintentionally overpower your partner. For singles, you may attract someone who is confident, passionate, and full of energy. This could be a powerful and dynamic connection but don't lose yourself in the excitement.

Health:
You need to take charge of your physical and mental well-being this month. Your enthusiasm and energy are excellent drivers, but also avoid burning out. Take a holistic approach to your health by focusing on both your body and mind. Find activities that fuel both your physical vitality and mental clarity, such as meditation, outdoor walks, or stress-relieving exercises.

Sagittarius (November 22 - December 21): Knight of Cups

Career & Finances:
The Knight of Cups brings a dreamy and idealistic energy to your career in December. You may be feeling inspired

to pursue a creative or artistic project, or perhaps you're driven by a desire to work in a field that aligns with your passions. However, it's important to remain grounded and practical as you move forward. Try not to overlook the practical aspects of your work or financial goals.

Love & Relationships:
If you're in a relationship, you may feel a surge of affection and romantic energy this month. It's a time to express your feelings openly and let your partner know how much they mean to you. For singles, the Knight of Cups portends a new romantic interest who sweeps you off your feet with charm, poetry, or intense emotional depth. Be careful not to get too carried away with idealized visions of love.

Health:
This month you may find that your emotional state directly impacts your physical energy and overall well-being. It's important to take care of your emotional needs by expressing your feelings and seeking support if needed. Be mindful of any emotional stress that could manifest physically.

Capricorn (December 22 - January 19): Queen of Wands

Career & Finances:
The Queen of Wands suggests that you'll be stepping into a position of influence, taking charge of your professional life with flair and determination. Your energy and enthusiasm will inspire those around you, and your efforts will likely lead to rewards. This is a great time to focus on your long-term goals, particularly those that require boldness and a creative approach.

Love & Relationships:
In relationships, the Queen of Wands brings warmth and excitement to your relationship. This is a good month to nurture your connection with your partner through fun activities or romantic gestures. For singles, it's a time to embrace your self-confidence and not be afraid to put yourself out there.

Health:
You are likely feeling energetic and motivated to take care

of your well-being. You may find yourself drawn to activities that enhance both your physical and mental health, such as exercise, yoga, or hobbies that spark your creativity. This is a month where you can really focus on your vitality and feel empowered to make healthy choices. Use this positive energy to boost your overall health and happiness.

Aquarius (January 20 - February 18): Six of Pentacles

Career & Finances:
The Six of Pentacles suggests that this month you may find yourself in a position where you're either receiving financial support or assistance from others, or you may be in a place to offer help or resources to someone else. There is an opportunity for mutual benefit. If you're dealing with financial issues, you are likely to receive the help you need, whether through a raise, a loan, or an unexpected windfall.

Love & Relationships:
In relationships, the Six of Pentacles indicates a need for

balance and reciprocity. Be mindful of any imbalances here as this can lead to potential conflicts and disappointments in the future. For singles, this is a good time for you to find someone who offers you emotional support and to whom you can also offer your presence as a gift.

Health:
This month, ensure that you're giving attention to all aspects of your health — physical, mental, and emotional. You may find that your overall well-being improves if you focus on making sure you're not overextending yourself or neglecting any area of your life. Remember to find a balance between work, rest, and personal time.

Pisces (February 19 - March 20): The Hermit

Career & Finances:
The Hermit in your career suggests a period of introspection and self-reflection. You may be taking some time off or stepping away from the hustle and bustle of everyday work to focus on your own personal growth or

direction. You may be guided to seek wisdom, either by consulting with a mentor or by spending time alone to reflect on your goals and aspirations.

Love & Relationships:
If you're in a relationship, you might feel the need for some space to reconnect with yourself. For singles, this could be a period of introspection, where you focus on healing and understanding your own needs before entering into a new romantic connection. The Hermit encourages you to find clarity within yourself before seeking it in others.

Health:
Take some time alone this month to recharge and reflect. You might feel the need to retreat from the world in order to focus on your well-being. This card encourages you to take time for rest, meditation, or quiet reflection. Pay attention to your mental health as well this month.

Conclusion:

December 2024 is a month of reflection, balancing priorities, and making choices across all areas of life. Whether you're deciding on career opportunities, reflecting on your relationships, or focusing on your health, the energy of the tarot cards suggests that this is a time to trust your intuition, embrace balance, and stay focused on your long-term goals. Take time to listen to your inner voice, and don't be afraid to make decisions that will align you with your highest purpose.

Wishing you a peaceful and fulfilling December!

About the writer

Meetu Sehgal is a Personal Transformation and Emotional Wellness Coach, EFT Trainer, Tarot Reader, Author, Reiki Grandmaster and Counselling Psychologist. With more than 15 years of experience in her field, she has been passionately working with individuals, helping them resolve health, wealth and relationship challenges through coaching. Meetu Sehgal is an MBA graduate from Delhi University and also holds a Masters in Psychology. Passionate about writing and spirituality, she has blended both in her work, which has helped hundreds of people around the world find peace within themselves. Her latest book, "Happy Inside Out", is a definitive guide to understanding and handling emotions and moods.

Spirit Speak

Wisdom through the ages

Words from the Wise by Rumi

This place made from our love for that emptiness!

Yet somehow comes emptiness,
this existence goes.

Praise to that happening, over and over!
For years I pulled my own existence out of emptiness.

Then one swoop, one swing of the arm,
that work is over.

Free of who I was, free of presence, free of dangerous
fear, hope,
free of mountainous wanting.

The here-and-now mountain is a tiny piece of a piece of
straw
blown off into emptiness.

These words I'm saying so much begin to lose meaning:
Existence, emptiness, mountain, straw:

Words and what they try to say swept
out the window, down the slant of the roof
~Rumi

Affirmation for the Month

"The end of a year is as good a time as any to release what no longer serves me."

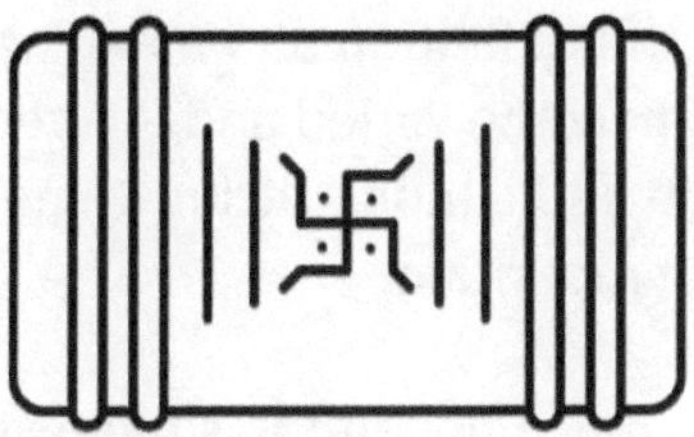

Rig Veda is one of the oldest literature ever written which consists of the explanation of the origin of the world, the power of Gods, and the art of living.

Sam Veda is considered to be the oldest music organisation in the world that contains all types of music, metre, mantra, chhanda, and linguistics.

Yajur Veda is a step-by-step guide to explain the right way of performing religious ceremonies and rituals and when one digs deeper into the Yajur Veda, one can find a deeper meaning than just the rituals.

Atharva Veda stands out among the other Vedas as it is the most diverse. It talks about occult science and also about death, spirits, and the afterlife.

About Ezine Kaleidoscope

In this new age, the definition and meaning of the word 'Spirituality' has become varied and is often misconstrued with fear, religion and a monk sitting in meditation on a lonely Himalayan mountain.

But spirituality is much beyond this faulty image. It is an inherent part of who we are. Because truly, we are spiritual beings having a human experience.

The purpose of Ezine Kaleidoscope is to bring the true essence of spirituality to our readers and make it so accessible that it doesn't feel like an alien overwhelming concept anymore. Our aim is to make it a part of everyone's everyday life.

If every living moment can be full of awareness, there will be joy and bliss in the world
-Meetu Sehgal

Ezine Kaleidoscope's journey began in November 2010 as a journey towards spirituality, awareness and making the spiritual tools accessible to all in a simple understandable manner.

It is our vision and mission to create awareness and remove the element of fear from spirituality and all things related. It is vested in light and that's what we want to bring to the life of everyone who reads us.

Know more about us

Website: ezinekaleidoscope.com
Email: info@ezinekaleidoscope.com
Instagram: @Ezine.Kaleidoscope
Facebook: www.facebook.com/ezineKaleidoscope

Subscription Details

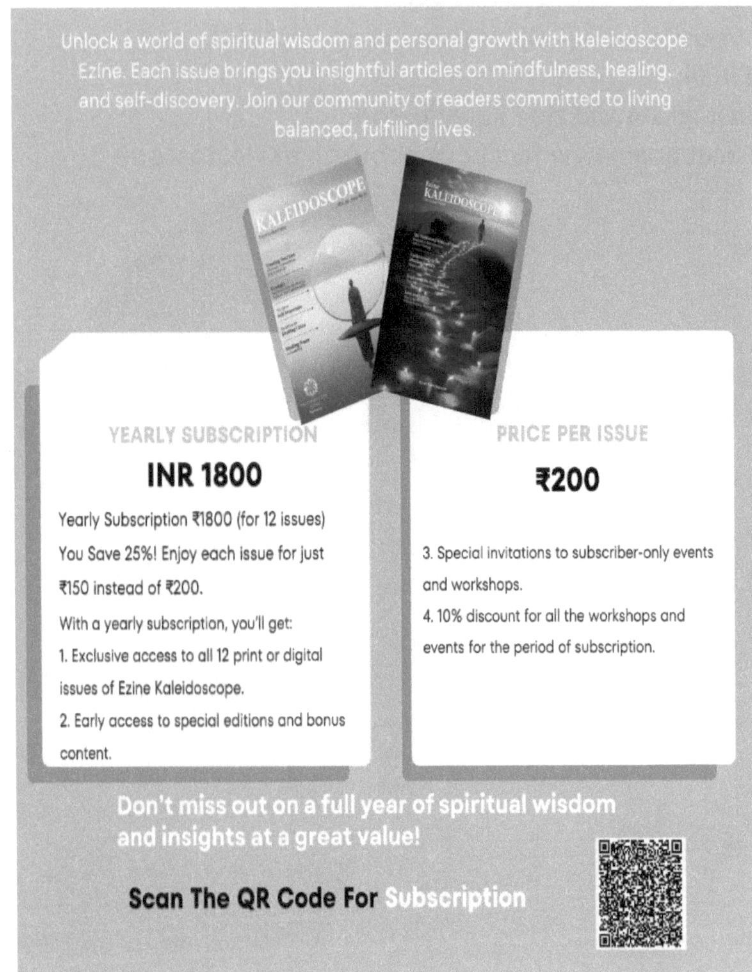

www.ingramcontent.com/pod-product-compliance
Lightning Source LLC
Chambersburg PA
CBHW031409250726
48656CB00002B/604